I was just laughing

Books by Thomas Timmins

Novels
> *Blood Medicine*
> *The Special Fruit Company*
> *Down at the River*
> *The Hour Between One and Two (Trilogy)*
> *Aphrodisiac for an Angel*

Short Fiction
> *Puff of Time*
> *Visions of My Other Self*
> *Desert Dusk Music*

Graphic Verse Novel
> *Zom*

Poetry
> *I Was Just Laughing*
> *Likings for Shadows*
> *Buddhist Breathing in America*

I was just laughing

Ghazals & Sonnets

THOMAS TIMMINS

ZOËTOWN MEDIA
HAYDENVILLE, MA

© 2016 Thomas Timmins
All rights reserved.

ISBN 978-0-9970287-0-6
Printed in the United States of America

Published by Zoëtown® Media
Zoëtown is a registered trademark of Zoëtown® Media.
Haydenville, MA
www.thomastimmins.com

Cover abstract digital painting Shutterstock
Book design by Maureen Moore, Booksmyth Press
www.thebooksmythpress.com

*For Claude and Shirley
who taught me to love a good laugh
just about more than anything*

Contents

Ghazals

Ghazal defined	13
The way of their mothers	14
If you have a gift of words	15
Prayers	16
A cold May	17
Accomplishment	18
Fragile waves	19
Trains	20
Legends of change	21
Northern cross	22
Missing the horses	23
Don't know what to do	24
Free woman	25
Just ride	26
Legacy	27
July duende	28
Passion	29
A whirring green ray	30
Angels without wings	31
Beautiful and sweet	32
Faux falls	33
Midsummer sunset	34
If I say "I"	35
The last thriller	36

Midsummer theft	37
An age of miracles	38
Sidewinding	39
Everyday child	40
70 flavors	41
True stories	42
Let's play	43
Wings	44
Lucky dog	45
Birds and people	46
Almost equinox	47
What to believe	48
The mysteries of human chemistry	49
Clouds and all	50
Leashes, reins, balls and chains	51
Refrigerator	52
Ms. Pleasure	53
Pie and luck	54
Voluptuous business	55
Thanksgiving	57
Hiking on a winter lake	58
Leave the lights on	59
Home	60
Gray skies	61
Indifferent world	62
"I was just laughing …"	63

Sonnets

Mums	67
You're my first memory	68
Brainy sonnet	69
Nothing, really	70
"Giants"	71
Boots and shovel	72
Dividing the assets	73
Wedding on the Southern Ocean	74
All Souls' Day	75
Her triumph	76
Balance	77
Krystal	78
Gnats and noseeums	79
Occupied	80
Friend phlox, cousin buttercup	81
Once one heart	82
Wee bird	83
On faith	84
The spider	85
Tugboat	86

Ghazals

Ghazal defined

The Arabic word ġazal is said roughly like the English word guzzle, but with the ġ pronounced without a closure between the tongue and soft palate, combined with a throaty h sound as in hustle, and with a light panting.

The ġhazal form appeals to me because its traditional subject matter concerns love, specifically an unattainable love for a person or the ineffable.

In its antique form, Urdu poets wrote in rhyming couplets with several other formal requirements. Each couplet formed its own poem, not necessarily related at first glance to the other couplets.

This reminds me of "leaping poetry," the idea popularized by Robert Bly in his book *Leaping Poetry* with its translations from Lorca and Neruda. The notion holds that images bridge the gap between the unconscious and the conscious. Ghazal stanzas form emotional and metaphorical islands, leaping from one to the other shaping archipelagos of sounds, images, feelings, ideas.

Over the last 800 years, the traditional ġhazal has evolved into various forms as poets have written ghazals in numerous languages. In *I was just laughing*, the couplets and triplets and longer stanzas sometimes rhyme, and they always leap interweave as they express love and other timeless mysteries like time, death, loss, and ecstasy.

The way of their mothers

In so many ways, men disappoint their mothers,
while daughters fear and mirror their mothers.

Evil exists in some people's hearts. Pity their ways.
They've not been redeemed by their mothers.

I rode only six and a half miles today,
but I pedaled fast all the way.

Now in jail, Jeremy dropped out of school at twelve,
he found his calling early – selling drugs was his way.

Many women without children have a mysterious way
of finding people and becoming their mothers.

In ancient China, seekers sought to live according to the Way.
That path started from nowhere and led them to their mothers.

If you have a gift of words

If you have a gift of words, and you do have a gift of words,
don't believe you're generous just because you go around speaking words.

It's Friday night, the work week has pulled your body's plug,
you feel drained until you hear her say, "I forgive you those careless words."

I asked the party, who has the pickles, who's got the corn? "Your old wife,"
my five year old grandson says, showing his gift with poetic words.

Patience is a virtue, says a book. She's an hour late. No matter.
I keep myself company by feeling up the gift of voluptuous words.

Whispers and cries, sounds only children and actors give voice to these days.
At the near and far edges of silence, what is the use of a gift of any words?

You want to know how crows and humans differ and resemble each other?
Feathers, flight and roadkill for crows. Fire, farming and folly for humans.
They both steal and have the gift of naughty words.

You have abundant beans and berries, Tommy, to nourish your gift of
words. When you know real hunger, you cherish a fusion of words.

Prayers

Biking by the canal at dusk, she spotted a brown cormorant, beak aimed
toward the sun, sitting on a guano-pinked boulder in the water.

I drove myself so hard and fast for years
the odometer in my brain spun loose, for all I cared.

Love has a way of talking with its fingers.
Idea: Each of us is a synaesthete if we'd pay attention. I wish I could.

Rotund prescription bottles line up in my medicine cabinet,
my stout amber squad poised to vanquish terrorists of pain and insomnia.

Paul never knew Jesus. King never knew Ghandi. Francis never knew the
ex-nun Debbie who runs hospice, or Debbie's 3 husbands and 7 kids.
Saints don't need to know each other, do they?

Now, Tommy, your mother taught you how to pray.
Keep her rosary by your bed, just in case. Go ahead, say it, if you want.
It can't hurt, can it? says the demon of solitude.

A cold May

Is it finally spring here in the hills?
Forsythia bloom beside victorious daffodils

though only pricker bush stalks bear leaves
while downy woodpeckers and purple finches peck their fill

at the feeder the evening before the black bear
saunters by and swats the feeder down. Still,

in the season again of avian and mammal mating, when love inspires hope,
I listen for words on the wind from my precious dead and those who killed

themselves for no hope. All remain silent as if they
forgot me, and of course they have, as you will forget,

Tommy, when your eyes close on the light
and bird trills and the soft padding of memories and the chill

of your bones returned to earth, your ghost of a heart the mystery it always
was in your chosen season, the infinite one beginning every April.

Accomplishment

If you want to talk about the mind, that's the least you can do.
If you feel what you feel, your heart lets you know what you can do.

I listen to the world's greatest music at the mere flick of a finger.
Am I a king? Nowadays, anyone with a few dollars can do the same thing.

Bach levitates from Segovia's fingers plucking wire strings on a wooden box.
A human world exists where people do far more
than we imagine we could ever do.

Every day, let's join the demonstration to exorcize
the demons from democracy by looking each other in the eye.
It's something we all can do.

It's getting later moment by moment, Tommy,
or have you stopped believing in time?
If you want, that's something else you can do.

Fragile waves

First fragile wave of dandelions bloomed and gone by already in the old pear
orchard, where years and years of blossoms and fruit have gone by already.

Wake up early and know who you'll be today so you can remember
the one you were on awakening, who by noon will be gone by already.

At tea yesterday, we sat on the couch remembering a loving friend who
disappeared into the fog, leaving us to wonder why she'd gone by already.

From the dense woods, cheery voices of sparrows and a thrush who, hearing
the purr of my cat, flew to safety, and now he's gone by already.

My friend, I'm waiting, a recluse waiting in sunshine,
sure I'll never stop longing for my beloveds who've gone by already.

Trains

Who knows if infinity exists?
Ideas like that can't be proven, even in this blooded body.

Sometimes silence hangs around the house, waiting.
Music, yes, music is welcome. Love songs and sweet nothings, too.

It's widely known, and acknowledged even by skeptics, each of us lives
in many worlds, always moving among them, mindlessly.

Did I concoct my painkilling cocktail tonight, or do I still need to?
It's no matter how much I want to be touched, I say. But it does.

The Bill of Rights assures us freedoms we don't know we have.
For example, a Minnesota judge doesn't have to hear cases
from South Sudan. Sometimes that's too bad.

Now, Tommy, the moon is waning. Next week, you'll take your
grandsons to the rail yard to watch the trains. You'll all crane your
necks and laugh, astonished at the beats of dieseling and the clangs and
clashes of switching, the ringing grinding banging of train thudding
and balancing on rails, wheel metal on rails screeching and whistling,
those great bulls of engines and bovine strings of cars so massive they
hammer the rails trembling the earth under your feet in a relentless
downbeat as they pass, everything shaking and groaning, dust rising,
then a little later, a little beyond, after they've gone, things settle down,
the earth and air calm down again and our hearts beat slow again, for a
while.

Legends of change

A friend told me he believed in deep change.
He's a pickpocket who snatches keys, wallets, and change.

Ancient now, she found herself in a room alone,
an only child once more, as if time brought no change.

Many women dancing with men dance alone.
Even at last released from whatever hut we lived in, can anyone change?

I love you, then I don't, I want to be alone.
Everything feels fine and then my feelings change.

Anyone, with food, light and warmth, can enjoy life living alone.
If we must, every one of us can hope to change.

Tomorrow, after breakfast, when I'm alone,
I'll lay around, do nothing but breathe and listen for a change.

Northern cross

Heading out for the Northern Cross
by the dark of the moon, she spreads her arms to the dark of the moon.

It all began in the sea, in the airless depths
where creatures emerged in love with the dark of the moon.

Shussss shhhhhh shhh rrrrr Atlantic shore.
Her feet rise as she slips into the water in the dark of the moon.

In the near field, a lone long-necked alpaca
guards his family hidden behind him inside the dark of the moon.

Children build fairy caves of small branches adorned with gay flowers.
They invite bright tiny fairies to come in from the dark of the moon.

These days have been long, long and wearying.
At last she rests, rests her bones and her being, here, in the dark of the moon.

Missing the horses

Woke up sad and weak this morning, missing the horses,
the grasses in the paddock growing wild, growing fast.

Somewhere on a sidewalk, in Cobble Hill, Brooklyn,
in the shade, a child smiles at her friend, offering him
a lick of her orange popsicle. He declines, preferring his own strawberry.

Is it allowed to speak of my son here in the desert,
where flesh and blood make all the difference, especially blood?

By the stream, six llamas grazing edge toward purple
loosestrife that insists it will never be fodder.

After a nap, he refused to rise until he was done dreaming
of the eight foot tall woman garbed in monk's brown robes
who was singing to him in a strange language only he could understand.

Now, Tommy, you can drive to town in your old car,
just make sure the brakes work and you have fluid in your steering system.

Don't know what to do

"Hey boss, I forgot what you said to do," the little workman said.
Then he laughed. "I don't mean in real life – it's a pretend game."

Don't deny it. You've never had a new idea, either. But we get along.
I don't know what to do. I don't know what to do.

When you kissed me, I believed in you.
When you cussed me, was it because I missed the turn to Lotus Land?

All this wondering and studying the wisdoms and poems
of the known greats – what does it matter if it doesn't make us laugh?

Now, Tommy, remember your mother who knew
what funny was. She'd want you to join the Laughing Club
that meets every noon on the town common, if you need to.

Free woman

The old boy asked me why I don't live with a woman.
I said I've tried it a few times, but she always left, that dear woman.

Around here, these days, we joke about how summer
comes before spring. It's like high times when I'm in love with a woman.

The soft earth turns green with praise for the sun,
the trees reveal their lusty buds, my heart is not lonely
but sometimes I feel hopeless love, like a mother's, a wise woman's.

I'm planning on throwing a party for artists and musicians
in my grassy yard like old times when my children ran and danced
around the Maypole with their aunt from the desert, the wild woman.

When I moved to the country, I stopped going out to the movies.
My car got old and time slowed down. I'm tempted
to make my own films, but I'll need help from an energetic, crazy woman.

She's right there, past the alpaca ranch and down the hill,
an easy ride on my bike. It took most of a lifetime, Tommy – now finally
you're a free man but you're still limited: you can only love a free woman.

Just ride

Nowhere to go but up and down hills, so just ride
I said. Come on, let's hop on our bikes and just ride.

When I was an infant my mother placed me on my belly
in bed where I learned to twist and bounce up and down and just ride.

My daily life used to feel like a roller coaster grinding up, shooting down.
I'm still in the coaster car but lately, I lean back and just ride.

Word has it nurses strike for higher principles, better pay,
better patient care. Ah, the power of principle.
With or without principles, it's easy to let everything just ride.

My young friend told me she couldn't take feeling so down much longer.
I didn't want to hear what she meant so I just let it ride.

Two boys on bikes schuss down a dry mountain streambed.
At the bottom, one told me, "I'm a Master. I just ride."

Today, Tommy, you woke, you drove, you sat, you drove, you ate, you
napped, you typed, you drank tea and coffee, you rose, then you pedalled
up Grassy Drive to the top of Bunny Hill, down Petuni Lane, leaving
every care at home, feeling fine the way you do when you just ride.

Legacy

The name of the mystery flower is the Canadian dwarf cinquefoil,
its gold petals glistening in clusters among green weeds,
                                        invulnerable to the drought.

When Mitch heard about the Quantum Flux, his eyes sparkled with pleasure
at the unpredictable, nervous energy shimmering
                                        inside of all of this.

My friend from the suburbs, fifty years after Allen found enlightenment
in the Safeway, you dressed in flowing peach silks and went shopping for
                                  blueberries and cream at the Stop & Shop.

My dad tries to never say "I" when he talks with someone.
He saves up the word "I" for you to spend on him a thousand times
                                        so you feel yourself loved.

Are you also an apostle of denial, that fabled first stage of grief?
I'd bet you are. Me, too. Otherwise, how could we wander this beloved
                                  world without endlessly weeping?

Now, Tommy, though the housefly has 4,000 lenses in each eye, you've killed
many, and like houseflies, your hungers for joy and love will never disappear.
                                      Your desires will be your legacy.

July duende

I thought the story was about me, but I was wrong.
It was about you, unless I'm wrong again.

The rusted yellow backhoe pulled into the barnyard
two days ago to dig the 37-year-old red mare's grave.

Her owner has brain cancer, but he's not worried for himself. It's his
son who lost his best friend, Peggy, the horse.

Here is the hole in the earth. Let's fill it with whinnies
about green meadows and good hay in the winter.

Maybe this isn't yours or my tale.
Maybe it's just another death song, the everyday kind.

Now, Tommy, soon you have to find a new place to live.
Make sure it has plenty of south-facing windows
and high ceilings and tall woods and green meadows around it.

Passion

My excuse for living the way I do holds
about as much water as an old colander, she said.

Late Saturday afternoon. Who's getting ready for church?
Who's staying in the lake, swimming the cool currents?

Hotel rooms have shrunk in Boston, Chinese tourists claim, while parking
garages dive deep underground and spiral up in vortexes into the sky.

I heard today we all need passion to succeed in life. As a boy, I learned the
Passion of Christ was Jesus whipped and oozing groaning to his crucifixion.

Peaches hang ripening on northern trees. Raspberries in the gardens
reward the town's black bears for being their famished selves.

Now, Tommy, it's not too late to fall in love, even if you ain't flush. In fact,
it's easier. Maybe that's why you're walking the broken side of the street.

A whirring green ray

I lose control of my heart when I listen in silence at dusk
to the girl with sea-green eyes who cries Celtic love songs at dusk.

Last night, or was it this morning? Nobody had flesh,
no hair, no mouth, no eyes, all bones jangling – no, it was at dusk.

Too few of us remember our dreams. During the day
they fade like shadows in our eyes at dusk.

Making our moves, finding our groove, it's play all day,
until soaked in our musk, our eyes fall closed at dusk.

Zipping in and out of his oleanders, the hummingbird's come to stay.
Out of the corner of my eye I spot him, a whirring green ray at dusk.

You want never to stop, Tommy, staying ever bright and fresh, until you
find yourself alone with your eyes damp and smarting at dusk.

Angels without wings

It is enough to bear learning the angels have lost their wings.
Who am I to say where or when or how the angels lost their wings?

The old man was a tough husband and strict father,
but his rough jaw sagged when he understood the angels lost their wings.

Bridges cross deep gorges aroar with headlong pounding crashing water
tearing at the mossy granite walls. Young men dive, smashing
into the foam heedless as angels who lost their wings.

Hot summer afternoons and nights people are not prone to seeing spirits.
If they see anything odd, it's only lonely angels who long ago lost their wings.

At 49, she became a mother for the first time,
to her 80-year-old father and 14-year-old niece. Her heart
soars in a world beyond the one where the angels lost their wings.

Beautiful and sweet

When you think about the power of night's shadows
and illusions, daylight seems flimsy, an inexorable delusion.

Carla still lives in the house where she cut my hair once,
as a favor, twenty years before Jim descended into
the grave, captive in Lou Gehrig's rusted armor.

We are trying to stay awake, demonstrating
consciousness to infinite mysterious forces we keep
trying to understand. This is called science.

A woman passed me on a bike. Something told me
it was an old girlfriend. Later, we met again.
It was her, wearing effervescent green, still beautiful and sweet.

In three days, two five-year-olds formed a construction
company, invented a new ball game, and finished a trike-athalon.
This is called the willpower of imagination.

Now, Tommy, you could have knelt with your knife
beside bouncy chard and frilly kale and gone to work
in the garden, but you lay down on the hillside, watching clouds.

Faux falls

Most of our planners
blueprint schemes and structures for happiness

as if knowing the shape of a tree
foretells its springtime ecstasy

or a faux waterfall in the desert pumped up through a ridge
and pouring down a red ledge

makes hikers as joyful
as a natural sluice rushing down a woodland gorge,

and it may, depending on circumstances,
and the time of day - the hotter the desert, the happier
the hiker coming on the faux falls.

You have nothing to fear, Tommy,
because you live where it rains and streams flow free,
all year round.

Midsummer sunset

Sunsets when you see lighting bolts flash in the south,
and a rainbow arch in the east
remind you you lucked out because you inhabit this body.

Talking on the phone late at night
is a habit I should break,
but I won't.

I need a bedtime story to help me sleep.
Always have, always will,
no chance I'll change now.

Please tell me a story about a world
that's even stranger than this one,
and let me make up my own happy ending.

Make love, it's good for you, with the right person,
of course, that beloved who might appear from behind you
in the checkout at the Mountainside Market.

Now, Tommy, the lightning could have started fires
and the rain slicked the roads,
but you gloried in tonight's tempestous sunset
and you smiled at everyone you met
and everyone smiled at you, glorying, too.

If I say "I"

If it feels like heaven blesses you,
why question it,
even if you are an unbeliever?

If I say "you," would you like it
if I say something true, or charming,
or would you rather I stay silent?

If I say "I,"
how long
before your eyes glaze over?

We are all in this together, you, oak trees, mule deer, me,
nematodes, rose quartz, flames.
If you agree, does it make you feel better or worse?

O my beautiful heart's desire, it doesn't matter we met,
then lost each other, then met again, I still miss you.
Do you long for me, too?

Now, Tommy, relax, settle down.
You can tell everything to your brother
if you can only find the words.

The last thriller

Three engineers told the mayor they could rebuild
the covered bridge. The river surged and trilled,
the citizens sang for the engineers.

Ninety percent of us won't change, weren't meant to
change, can't change our given minds,
so we age, with wrinkles and aching hands, becoming something new to
ourselves, whether we accept it or not.

His thriller novel open beside him, my dad died
alone in his bed. He had a fine day, laughed
with grandson Johnny, saw people he loved,
had serious talks and told jokes, some salty, some sweet.

Still, things didn't work out as they planned.
They were going to get better and go home together.
Of the countless questions to ask, Tommy,
ask the one about how to die in ecstasy.

Midsummer theft

Traveling to the far place where when you enter,
you stop your tongue and keep it still.

Men and women fall out of love again and again.
The lucky ones remain friends in love.

When he aimed his eyeballs toward mine, he didn't
look me in the eye because his forehead got in the way.

"I've been the leaver, I've been the left.
Ain't the one the easier, both some kind of theft."

We're the open-hearted kind, you and me.
What's mine is yours, what's yours is mine.

Tommy, you feel good you set up an email account tonight.
Now, who will you write?

An age of miracles

The downpour arrived too soon, in a hurry,
a drunken uncle you'd just as soon not see.

Yesterday, steam swirled off the shed roof
rising, disappearing into the blue nostril of sky.

If you have ever bowed to Buddha
you could also say a rosary to the Holy Mother.

A Chinese woman bodybuilder migrates to the United States leaving
behind her hiphop star son in Beijing. She pummeled my back and legs
until I yelled. "O," she said, "is that too hard?"

A recent theory of love claims it's pink or brown or white.
Mix them together, what do you get? Toast with cinnamon and sugar.

Of course, you're going to die, like everyone here and all
who went into the next world before you, Tommy.
You'll keep your faith in love, since we know we live in an age of miracles.

Sidewinding

Did you forget it's the nature of knees
to flex and extend no matter how stiff or swollen?

As Megan curled and snaked and poured her body across the floor,
why were you surprised the lights dimmed even more
and your eyes began to tear up and your heart rose into your throat?

Everyone's tired, the President's tired,
the Masters of War champion is tired.
It's only lunchtime, and everyone's tired.

Please, don't worry again tonight. You'll sleep
or you won't. Tomorrow's coming is what really matters.
At last and always, the sadness flourishes and the healing begins.

It sidewinds through the twilight breeze.
Now, Tommy, go ahead, give yourself 30 days
of happiness, for no reason. If that's not enough time, take more.

Everyday child

The everyday child singing to himself
races around exploring the world beyond himself.

Bent into the wind, pacing icy sidewalks,
he pounds on the door, seeking her for himself.

He says, hurl the ball with your left hand if you can.
If you don't, he says he'll pitch it himself.

Five months from now I'm standing on top of the Mt. Toby firetower
with three friends who hiked up with me: he, him, and himself.

It's useless to give himself pep talks
when he's already pleased with gossip he hears and repeats to himself.

When gifts surprise us, let's accept them with gratitude
or the one who gave them may take them back and keep them all to himself.

Did you forget, Tommy, you can receive true gifts
when you need them so bad you almost give up?
Whoever gives them to you also gives them to himself.

70 flavors

He finally connected his inner life with his outer.
It felt like joy, this singing
the saddest ballad he knew.

While the baby runs naked in the yard,
the women talk and feed the men grilled fish
and peace they can find nowhere else.

Buckminster Fuller said
the formula for the number of relationships
you have in a group is N2 x N over 2. N is the number of beings.

What about the relationships I have
with my many selves?
Do they count?

When rain came again tonight, we decided
to eat soft serve in the car.
The Creamee offered 70 flavors, but we tried only two,
three if you count chocolate/vanilla swirl as two.

Now, Tommy, take a pill if you need one to sleep,
because you have to get up early for work in the morning.
This is not work, but maybe it should be?

True stories

Remember the old cartoon with the man, can opener
in hand, trying to pry open his head? Ugly, sure. Funny?
He was looking for his mind. He thought it was inside his head.

A woman told me what she said was a true story
about a little boy who believed the world
was his magic carpet. He flew from sunrise to sunset, then he slept.

And she told me another true story
about an old man who used to fly carpets
before he bought an orchard and settled down to raise peaches and plums.

I'm all ears for any story you want to tell me
as long as it's true. And how will I know if it's true?
You'll tell me, won't you?

The woman who knows a thousand true stories
bore a daughter who sang a thousand love songs
and a son who loved a thousand women, true or false?

So much for philosophy and tall tales.
Now how much would that be? That's right, Tommy,
pick a card, any card, any card will do.

Let's play

for Amy

You said I'm fun and you like fun so I said, let's play.
In the old concrete leaky lakeside rec building, a spooky place but fun,
we picked up the ping pong paddles and you said, let's play.

I tried to make up new rules for silly fun
and even though I couldn't understand my new rules, I said let's play.
You agreed you'd stay happy if the game was fun.
You laughed and sliced the ball into the corner
and I said, okay, let's really play.

We couldn't have had more fun
or felt such victory as when we moved to the pool table
and you dropped three balls in a row
into three different pockets after I said, hey, wanna play?

You're my game, you're my fun
so if you're ready, what do you say? Let's play.

Wings

We returned to the woods from a three-day journey
through the dizzy land of the casino.
Today's a Saturday morning resurrection.

Somewhere in my family DNA, a Christian
sings the Sermon on the Mount,
the only words in the Book that matter to me.

Across the web, Mozart thrills anyone who needs,
who dares to listen. In every note, he sacrificed his life,
as if he had no cares about legacy.

Little Billie watches me with pensive, smiling eyes.
I have her photo on my wall to help me keep my head
out of the sand.

Admit it, Tommy, your dreams when you fly without wings come true
when you love. Nothing else in this world
brings you such exhilaration.

Lucky dog

She swiveled her hips and sang harsh words about suffering women
and abuse. The audience knew they'd never know Brooklyn like she did.

I'm running out of patience, I pity my body for its enduring pain.
I used to feel a little discomfort or even weariness. Now it lingers.

Here in the north country, we don't like to admit we're in the north country.
Melting snow doesn't mean it's spring anymore.
It's springtime somewhere south of here.

My sister didn't know what a treat a colonoscopy
can be until they mainlined her with Versed,
"Divine nectar for any soul," she said, "in any state of grace."

Morning. A few quiet moments before work.
Some mornings I dread, some I merely fear.
This morning I feel pretty good.

Your true friend promised
she'd always be there for you, Tommy. You lucky dog.
You've always loved her and she's never told a lie of the heart.

Birds and people

When the sun this morning woke up the town,
it excited more than the birds and people.

Here we are, you and I, you here, I back in town.
We've heard strange stories about more than birds
and much more than people.

You asked me, who lives outside of town, why did I go to Ford's Theater,
other than for the birds in my body
and in my mind, the people.

The answer lies in the toe-trapping beats of life in that city
where its dreams, its machines, its vivid greens, its wilderness
of beasts all looked kindly on birds and people.

Why then is "why" less a city word and more a town word,
where "because" evaporates as it nears the birds and people?

You're not the candyman, Tommy, you're not the mayor
of the town. At your best, you praise birds and love people.

Almost equinox

Before I go to the movie, I wonder if I'll like it,
& if I do, why? Do you ever wonder that?

He said they'd go for a long ride.
When I came home, their bikes were still parked in the garage.

David writes to provoke people to do something big.
His words are music, his images are sunlight condensed. He's dangerous.

Did you make the right decision, he asked me.
I'm not ready to throw a parade about it, I said, but I think so.

Stuff is the easiest thing to deal with
if you don't have much when you split up.

There's a new lilt to your step, heel and toe, heal and toe,
less tilt, less limp in your knee. The weather has dried up, cooled off.

What to believe

Dear young friend, how much new do you get from the News?
Does what you learn help you tie your shoes?

Have you felt this year's young autumn sprites
plying your senses with crystal daylights, long sleepy nights?

"Forty years ago" is something I want to write
a hundred years from now, fit of body, mighty of mind, who knows how.

Do you expect penmanship to become
anything more than an antique art form?

Oh, dear, I do love to shout out my opinions, like anyone,
not trying to convince you, act superior, just to have a little fun.

Now, Tommy, when you speak about yourself as if you knew who you were,
please don't believe everything you say, it's only words.

The mysteries of human chemistry

Was is Krishna, Christ,
or a cotton-brained boy who said
"What is Love?"

Back in the wilds of the last century, she sang
love was a second-hand emotion.
We wondered what was the first-hand emotion?

The "Word was made Flesh" has it backwards.
Are not my tongue, lips, teeth, and cheeks
the flesh words come from?

Breath, the mother of flesh, is mistaken for the Word.
Breath also makes song, groan, chatter, wail
and the aching murmurs of love.

We used to call it longing, or if deep and painful enough, heart's desire.
Now, those in the know say
it's pheromones, dopamine, and oxytocin.

We pursue the mysteries of human chemistry,
but so few have any talent for the lab.
Did you know, Tommy, this life is all lab,
and the only experiment worth doing is cultivating love?

Clouds and all

They came again at ten o'clock at night.
I'd wanted them to visit me
for months, so I said "Welcome"

and here they are, empty-handed,
mindless, now disappearing into the October woods
like the dreams of children they are.

And you – do they come to you
before you fall asleep? If they do,
do you pin them down or ignore them

since paying too close attention to them
will reveal longings you must keep secret
or you'll jinx your getting away.

You know, and I know, it's about desire
passing across a late afternoon like sundogs
posing to the south and north of the sun.

What memories are you hiding, Tommy?
Because so many of your beloveds have gone
leaving you with the sky, your fast friend, clouds and all.

Leashes, reins, balls and chains

She's a jungle of impulses she can barely control.
In her dreams, she cultivates impulse control.

Deep in the hidden greenhouse named Beckoning Gardens
blooms an orchid named Impulse Beyond Control.

Under a lofty prairie sky,
Norwegian farmers steward the "land under their control."

Black earth left alone ripens into long grasses,
then grains and pulses surrender to sun and rain's control.

She reads late into the night, "romantic smut."
In the fantasy world she gives in to her impulse to abandon all control.

The way to be free of leashes, reins, balls and chains,
is to lose fearful desire, Tommy, to not worry it's all out of control.

Refrigerator

When you live with other people,
family or friends, the refrigerator

stays as much a mystery as people are.
I keep to the front edge of the shelves of the refrigerator

and maybe of people,
too, who, unlike a refrigerator

don't just stand there chilling. People
move left and right, they close and open like a refrigerator

door revealing surprises and leftovers. People like you, Tommy,
take too much solace from your midnight refrigerator.

Ms. Pleasure

She's real, this woman,
the beautiful, the fragrant, the soft.

The juicy songbird of morning joy,
the infinite shades of rainbow promises.

She laughs and says she doubts it.
She tells the truth as no one else sees it.

Let's eat, let's not eat, let's drink, forget the booze.
Let's celebrate by lying down. Do you think I'll sleep?

Soon it will be me rocking in a porch chair
calling out to that woman who winks, flaunts her wrinkles.

Twist me up, shake me down, abandon me,
I'll never let you go, Ms. Pleasure, my woman, my life.

Pie and luck

At eighty-nine, Mom, your stricken brain
lets your mind fly. Your bright eyes tell us you'll soon
catch up with the man you call Claude.

A friend who used to be a believer told me
if I wanted to be saved
I should learn how to bake pumpkin and apple pies.

It wasn't I didn't want to kill – nobody does –
or even feared to die, I was just lucky enough to ignore
what the herd's wisdom demanded.

Notice how dark it is, Tommy, even before
Daylight Savings time. If you're lucky tonight,
some one you love will kiss your lips and rub your head.

Voluptuous business

It's nearly November
when the voluptuous business
of making summer babies begins.

In bed,
the Republicans believe
their will should rule.

At the bank,
the Democrats don't worry
about whose money it is.

Mr. Qi Nen, Ms. Culpepper, Senor Carruddi,
Madame Rose Sans Neuf,
leave your children home but don't leave them home alone.

Little Juancho, you and I will forget
our magnificent dinner
with the beautiful mothers

because even then our longing for love
dulled every sensation of pleasure and beauty,
the source of our happy memories.

Beyond the arid farms of either-or and
down inside the river of if-then where
the patience of water meets the stubbornness of the sun,

everything aches and the aches cry out
from the throats of men and women
god, my god, how could I feel

so free, so happy, so crazy like
right now is this all I could ever want?
Yeah yeah, sure, yes, yes, no, no, o, o, yes ... yes.

Thanksgiving

How is it tonight feels so warm? Snow on the ground this morning
made us turn up the thermostat to stay warm. Could we all find
our talents like we find ourselves in beds some afternoons with a lover?

A useful tip from the road:
The Law of the First Leg: warming up.
It takes 50% of the entire journey's energy output

to complete the first 10% of the journey, measured in time.
Still, the first steps can decide the ultimate realities
of the entire journey, especially the journey of lovers.

The bland tofu you cooked this morning became a rich, sweet, salty,
warming gingery, garlicky, surprising, enlivening feast,
complete with sake and other dining comestibles.

As if eating such hearty fare
was consuming a lover while at the same time
being consumed by her seasalt scents and pungent flavors.

Hiking on a winter lake

When you can get things done by desire,
not working or spending energy,
then you have nothing to worry about.

Hiking across a winter lake reminds me of holding hands under pale
winter sun with Donna Ray, my beloved when we were fourteen,
each wearing warm gloves and skidding across a frozen slough.

In the white leather back seat of Toney's dad's
blue Cadillac convertible, we cuddled our girls
and rubbed, giggling, nipping, puffing like teenage puppies.

They say pain from kidney stones hurts like birthing,
but that's not true. Bearing forth a pebble hurts,
but it's simple, soon over and done.

So many people I know well these days,
except my children, could be grandparents,
by fortune or by age.

By now you understand, Tommy. Strange things come around when
you don't expect them, and good luck
happens when you go out and mosey along the canal.

Leave the lights on

Hey, slow down, friend, no use getting in trouble
or a ticket now. The road is long and it's almost dark.

We ain't going nowhere trouble is today or tomorrow
and I want to see your sparkle eyes before dark

closes in and hides your face in shadows.
That's why we have to stop now, before it gets dark

all over town. My old photos of your eyes show
they're soft and blinky at dawn and sea blue and deep after dark.

Remember, Tommy, the trouble your curiosity
can cause today when you switch off the lights just at dark.

The sudden loss of light frightens the children so they stay awake
late into the night. Leave on the lights so we can all enjoy the dark.

Home

As you turn the car toward home,
the blinker clip clops around the corner, the pony nearly home.

Mirrors line the hallway walls like pressed pearls,
a cold elegance not found in many homes.

The most favorite word in the world's tongues
must be "mother." Next come the names for "home."

For two years I've been subterranean, an underground
man, dwelling in a basement. Mid-winter light calls, light
draws me out, light pulls me close to home.

The Christmas cactus won't bloom in the dark living room.
My mother's amaryllis blooms with nine flowers in the
south sun of her final home.

Some few feel their way through the world, confident, smiling, optimistic.
Most fidget, dash, or dawdle their way, hungry
for a tiny taste of long lost home.

"People tell us we'll move south when we retire," she said.
"Not a chance, I tell them. I want to stay home.
I want to enjoy my home."

Since you left your childhood home, Tommy, you've not called anyplace home.
If you'd let somewhere claim you, you'd defend it.
Go ahead. Fall in love with your home.

Gray skies

When we can barely stay awake under daily gray skies,
coffee and endorphins might wake us up to the beauty
inside steel gray skies.

When you don't know someone well, you can mention the forecast
and a swell conversation can start, anywhere under the sun
or dark gray skies.

It's not the snow, the sleet, the one gray day,
but the weeks of shadows when our eyes long
for golden light to pierce through dense gray skies.

Gray skies excuse us to hide under the covers,
to play the bear, to take comfort in our fat bellies,
to mime in silence dim days delivered by gray skies.

You could move south, Tommy,
where light lasts longer
and gray skies

bring relief. Would you rather bear the drought
endless sun inflicts, or floods and fertile rain promised
by heavy gray skies?

Indifferent world

You have every right to want out of this indifferent world
though you're anchored here by your loved ones in this painful world.

People worried about this early spring, as if bare-legged warmth
and early budding are too fragile to love in this northern world.

You took off the other day exploring a forbidden place,
a secret place of light you've always loved in this heavy world.

If you hadn't returned, how could we ever forgive ourselves for not
holding you inside our vigilance in this terrifying world.

Even a hint of happiness, a distant birdcall, a swath of sunlight
can wet the tragic soil of our love for this wintry world.

It's spring, Tommy, the fabled season of hope and
optimism, a time you fear will drive your friend
beyond your heart's reach, gone from this agonic world.

"I was just laughing …"

Our frail old mother said, "I was just laughing …"
These were her final words:
"I was just laughing …"

After lunch, she lay on her bed, eyes closed,
not napping, tickled by something, a memory, a vision, a pleasure.
She couldn't help herself from just laughing.

She couldn't help herself walk either,
or hear someone else speak quietly
unless they were just laughing.

Last Halloween, she and I, laughing ourselves to tears,
watched lunatic TV food sculptors,
we howled and cried far beyond just laughing.

You took comfort, Tommy, in her last words, remembering Jerry Lewis
said, "It ain't funny unless there's some sad in it."
Now she's gone, she's gone, even if at the end, she was just laughing.

Sonnets

Mums

"Mums," you whispered, or was it "Mom's?"
I eased into my bone age when she whispered

"Let me touch you down into your skin now,"
always gentle thrilling me, filling

my new mouth with honeysuckle-sweet nectars –
"blessings" I learned to call them,

after I'd lost their original silk
taste, and let my thirsting tongue seek its milk
havens in sugar, salt, song, in freedom
of bright words, soft kisses. Or did I hear

"Roses?" Feeling myself bouyed up, afloat,
yes, gliding through a roses's glowing heart,
meandering a fragrant world you make bloom.
"Mums?" No. "Mom's?" No . Blown roses. Heart's perfume.

You're my first memory

You're my first memory. I don't know where
but I played alone with a little chair.
You must have been only twenty-three
or four when, tall as the ceiling, you walked in
and rolled the basketball across the floor
to me. I crawled up and bellied over
the big ball, warm from your hand. Your talking
with Mom, in words soundless now, then spoken
as a song thrilling in my baby's ears,
filled the room overhead with trillings
I could see when I raised up my eyes to hear
and watch your face from below your knees. Dear
Dad, in this world you are my first memory.
Forty years, and your voice still sings for me.

Brainy sonnet

Your left brain is down on its knees
begging your right brain to speak clearly
its love and threatening to jump all over it
if it doesn't start responding in a way
the left brain can understand

while your right brain hums
a new tune it might just sing out at dawn
when the bacon sizzles and the coffee steams
and the new recipe for bliss floats up
from the meadow on the mist.

Neither of your brains knows the other
but they've gotten along all these years
because they're Siamese twins with different parents,
so what else could they do?

Nothing, really

I saw your handsome mug today
in the brochure Non-Violent Peace Force
sent to donors and would-be donors like me.
You looked pale, bro, standing beside the helicopter

with a friend, ready to depart, wearing a dark slouch hat
under the South Sudan sun. Maybe from too much light?
Maybe too much violence everywhere you try and try
to make non-of.

You were smiling your ambivalent smile, the one
I first saw on your face when they'd tossed
your young radical self into the hoosegow
and poured more drugs into you than you'd ever take

yourself. It's your smile that says, Yeah,
this is a big deal, but it's nothing, really.

"Giants"

Hidden in the drying grass
dry dirt heaped by a visiting mole.
No one has ever seen the mole,
only its tracings.

Hidden in her shaded room
she waits out the late afternoon sun.
No one knows how tired
the sun makes her feel.

No one will ever know. Why should she tell
because it doesn't matter once
the long shadows appear.

Only she and a few children notice
as they play "giants"
with their shadows on the grass.

Boots and shovel

My boots are stuck in the clay.
Digging out, my shovel makes my wrists ache.
If the sky would listen, I have plenty to say.
I don't know if today's sun's real or fake.

Planting a big garden, not just for greens,
tho I love fresh red chard and buttery lettuce.
For spice, add pickled onions and beets.
I worry about water, some say soon there's not enough
even for people to drink.

My shovel don't talk or grunt like I do,
but under my boot it slices through mud and roots.
Me and the shovel we ain't birds of a feather
but its head and my feet work just fine together,
neither of us bother to think.

Dividing the assets

Glossy, gray granules glued together
into ordinary square of grilled hamburger

flopped over the circular rim of a pale bun,
etched with pattern frayed as an old carpet

no one notices on the pantry floor
during the family post-mortem division of assets

Aunt Lucy neglected to assign
when she willed "anything he needs or wants

for as long as he lives" to Sam, her two-year old cat.
All eyes were on silver-waved Dave,

the portly attorney who would never avoid
a juicy burger even in this age of lettuce and tomato.

"Pile on the mayo," he says, "extra mustard, too.
And, please, folks, let's not skimp on those fries."

Wedding on the Southern Ocean

Clustered penguins flick salt from stubby wings.
As they pass by mirrors, their throats warble
their doubts about this party's off-shore sobriety.
The Captain's two daughters, after all,
don't marry every day, especially these
auburn-locked girls, he, the skipper,
tall in glossy black wool and spit-polished leather,
will give away today.
"By god," he booms, "released
from my dominion," by the husbands,
boys really, paupers still, but the Old Man knows
they bear emerald and diamond crescents
embossed in all their charts: nautical, natal, sidereal.
The Captain chuckles. Penguins waddle across the deck.

All Souls' Day

Alone for the first time in months,
except for a small fire
flickering orange & black behind
the wood stove's clear glass door.

Alone, but not really. Friends text me,
and I read their words, some solace,
some boring, none worrisome today.

Sitting alone as I've longed for,
in my home, a makeshift space,
but safe & quiet for as long as the lease lasts,
months from now.

Then, desire for your touch arises.
So I imagine your kissing me, then I drink another coffee,
and go out to fetch more wood.

Her triumph

The Triumph she rides
is her whole hog,

her sole hog,
no surrogate for being,

no proxy for a soft thing
on her mind.

The bike,
winged power,

tilting and banking,
ripping and rolling,

it's her bike,
her ride,

her growl,
her glide.

Balance

When a single tree or a grove in the forest
falls ill, the healthy trees
send carbon and nitrogen transfusions
through roots and underground streams
to the troubled trees until they heal.

Our outer worlds
and inner worlds
always creating each other

balance not as light and dark,
those spirits of air,
illusions of the eyes,

but like the trees'
mutual nourishment and healing –
they are inseparable, inevitable, essential.

Krystal

"Krystal," I called into the past, "Krystal."
Six two and ten years older, thirty at least,

thirty two. Only because I loved her,
she gave me a laughable

B-minus, though I was the best verdammt
speaker, drunk or clear-headed,

in the whole German class. She taught me
how to remember: Given the A I deserved, I'd

forget her, but I'm still trying to please
my beloved with the long legs and tangled hair rolled

into a bun. Watching me – Watch close, Krystal,
see me, bold as thunder – she raises black eyebrows,

delicate as dark ears of a fox on patrol,
her ebony eyes flashing, watching me, listening.

Gnats and noseeums

Where sky hung low, cloud tails dripping shreds
of cold steam on cattails' unwavering
upraised noses, in a bog whose
name no one remembers, whose pert lilies
swear bright orange passion for the stream
seeping down under their green sloughy bed –
at such a place, gnats and nosee-ums thrive.

Seeking nurture, innocent of the fate
of birds' beaks, wearing a full morning's weight
of water on their wings, they sting, dig, burrow
the flesh of egret, raccoon, and mine.

By noon, sweat lays sour on my skin, cream
poured and curdled by sky itself. My arms
flap cool puffs of breeze the bugs ride away.

Occupied

for Jasmin and Caraway

When your mother and I had to show
our I.D.s to get back onto our block from work
or shopping, the National Guard
roamed the streets in two's on foot, or they lurked
on dim corners, cadging flirty glances
from cool girls, girls like you now, shining soft girls
whose hair and skirts flowed like the smoky dances
happening up at Tule Lake: bare legs whirl,
ruby lips curl, shadowy bodies meander
through the firelit, twilight park
as free and safe as deer in the wildlife preserve.
Those boys with guns gawked, wanting, having lost
the nerve a gentle touch takes, so they sat, tough, shy
polishing rifles clenched between camo thighs.

Friend phlox, cousin buttercup

Friend phlox, cousin buttercup, in a wild
mood my fingers followed a perfumed trail
among soft chartreuse leaves that kissed my hands
like kittens' tongues licking. Then I picked at random
choosing a few stems to come back
with me to class in the jail where, off track,
hedged in by thorned concertina, roughed up
young men with fragile minds, wild hearts, sloughed off
by the world of cookies, tea and roses,
cluster in shadowy rooms, their losses
bloomed like you, phlox, with rampant memories
of bright hillsides they tumbled across, free
to rise or fall. Like you, gold buttercup,
with your million seeds, their longing never stops.

Once one heart

Once one heart beat in both our breasts,
love arrived for good, and all fear fled.

It's no matter now the lives we lead keep us apart.

My one heart pulses solo,
missing beats, wanting touch, dreaming play.

Some say love's not enough after all,
without luck and time, jewels and home.

With us, if luck, it was the luck of fate.
We met. We loved. We pledged our love.

Besides sun and rain, what else in the world
could my one heart want?

Don't let me now mulling in sorrow lie to myself or you.

My heart wants one thing only – to beat once more
as one with yours and never again to stop.

Wee bird

A secret brook whose tilted stone stair-stepped
falls reveal deep sedimentary shock
long ago, surely before humans set
foot along this stream where now a spongy
moss softens the rocky ledge, iridescing
the stone. Moist beds for hemlock seedlings,
lush feeding grounds for a perk-tailed wren who
flits and pokes, a levitated chipmunk,
searching branch and twig snagged in upturned roots,
his bright five-bar song fluting out, leaping
upstream. Silvery notes fiddle and float
the tender breeze as if fizzy bubbles
leapt up green-slanted sun beams and popped, ringing
liquid bells in the wee bird's jeweled throat.

On faith

The path to the graveyard
everyone walks in high hopes
past the crossroads just ahead
that leads to the ranch

where the Sky Stallion waits for us
to mount his broad back,
so he can carry us far away
beyond this, beyond that,
beyond our wildest imaginings.

We know he's there, not far away.
There's no doubt about it.
We can see the flies
and smell the horseshit
steaming on the road ahead.

The spider

In the damp end of the drying old stream,
a round orange body of a spider
floats above a rotted sawn stump, its starred
root end clumped up with sticks and leaves washed
down last spring. That last storm, this dryer than sand
summer, left some wet under stones, haven
from sun in the dark. The sun's sere breeze stirs
 a fine mist up, blowing it meadowwards
where new mown hay perfumes a dozy day,
as the spider glows – tiny sun deep in the woods,
its legs nearly invisible shadowy rays –
and watches a flurry of woods bugs swarm.
The spider – death's ally in its patience.
In its hunger, life's mastery of death.

Tugboat

Trailing a wide wake,
I urge barges, busted mast riggers,
fancy yachts with drunken captains
going nowhere without
a big shove from my broad shoulders.
They call me the ox of the bay.
I plow currents, I carve waves.
Able to handle ships
ten times larger, and a hundred times larger
when we yoke ourselves into
teams, some pulling, some pushing,
all linked across oily, riled water,
aiming for the deeps where
I return power to the ships'
masters for their long journeys into unknown seas.

www.ingramcontent.com/pod-product-compliance
Lightning Source LLC
Chambersburg PA
CBHW021135300426
44113CB00006B/434